Pebble®
Plus

ICE AGE ANIMALS

Arctic Shrews

by Joy Frisch-Schmoll

Consulting Editor: Gail Saunders-Smith, PhD

Content Consultant: Margaret M. Yacobucci, PhD
Education and Outreach Coordinator,
Paleontological Society; Associate Professor,
Department of Geology, Bowling Green State University

Raintree is an imprint of Capstone Global Library Limited, a company incorporated in England and Wales having its registered office at 7 Pilgrim Street, London, EC4V 6LB – Registered company number: 6695582

www.raintree.co.uk
myorders@raintree.co.uk

Editorial Credits
Jeni Wittrock, editor; Peggie Carley and Janet Kusmierski, designers; Wanda Winch, media researcher; Laura Manthe, production specialist

ISBN 978 1 4062 9364 7 (hardback)
18 17 16 15 14
10 9 8 7 6 5 4 3 2 1

ISBN 978 1 4062 9371 5 (paperback)
19 18 17 16
10 9 8 7 6 5 4 3 2 1

British Library Cataloguing in Publication Data
A full catalogue record for this book is available from the British Library.

Photo Credits
Illustrator: Jon Hughes
Shutterstock: Alex Staroseltsev, snowball, April Cat, icicles, Leigh Prather, ice crystals, LilKar, cover background, pcruciatti, interior background

Printed and bound in China.

Contents

Small survivor

A tiny creature darts through the weeds. It spies a grasshopper and pounces! It catches the insect and eats it. Then the furry hunter hurries on.

Shrew bodies

An arctic shrew is one of

the world's smallest mammals.

A shrew has a long tail

and a pointed snout.

Its eyes and ears are tiny.

Shrews have been around for millions of years. When other animals died out during the Ice Age, arctic shrews survived.

Grassy home

Today arctic shrews live in Canada and the northern United States. They like grassy wetlands such as marshes and swamps.

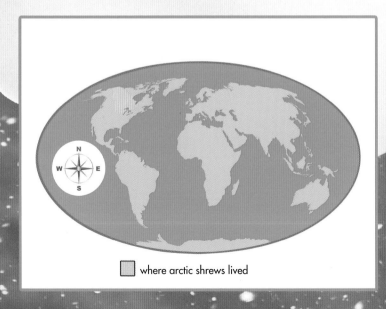

where arctic shrews lived

Arctic shrews build their homes in old stumps and under logs and rocks. Their nests are made of dried grass, leaves and moss.

Time to eat

Shrews are always hungry. They must eat every few hours to stay alive. Hunting day and night, they search for insects, snails and worms.

Sniff! Shrews find insects with their noses. They catch insects with their sharp teeth. Shrews can eat their own weight in food every day!

A short life

A female shrew usually has two litters a year. She gives birth to four to nine babies. The babies are born blind and have no fur.

When young shrews can care for themselves, they live alone. They do not like to be with other shrews. Shrews live for up to 18 months.

Glossary

Ice Age time when much of Earth was covered in ice; the last ice age ended about 11,500 years ago

litter group of animals born at the same time to the same mother

mammal warm–blooded animal with hair or fur; female mammals give birth to live young and feed them milk

marsh area of low, wet land

snout long front part of an animal's head; it includes the nose, mouth and jaw

swamp area with trees that is partly covered by water

Read more

The Ice Age Tracker's Guide, Adrian Lister and
Martin Ursell: (Frances Lincoln Children's Books, 2010)

Prehistoric Life (Eyewitness), William Lindsay
(Dorling Kindersley, 2012)

The World's Smallest Dinosaurs (Extreme Dinosaurs),
Rupert Matthews, (Raintree, 2013)

Websites

www.bbc.co.uk/nature/ancient_earth/Last_glacial_period
Watch videos and find out more about these fascinating
ice age.

www.bbc.co.uk/nature/life/Common_Shrew
Learn more about shrews – where they live now, and
the dangers they face today!

Index